# *WHAT ARE YOU?*

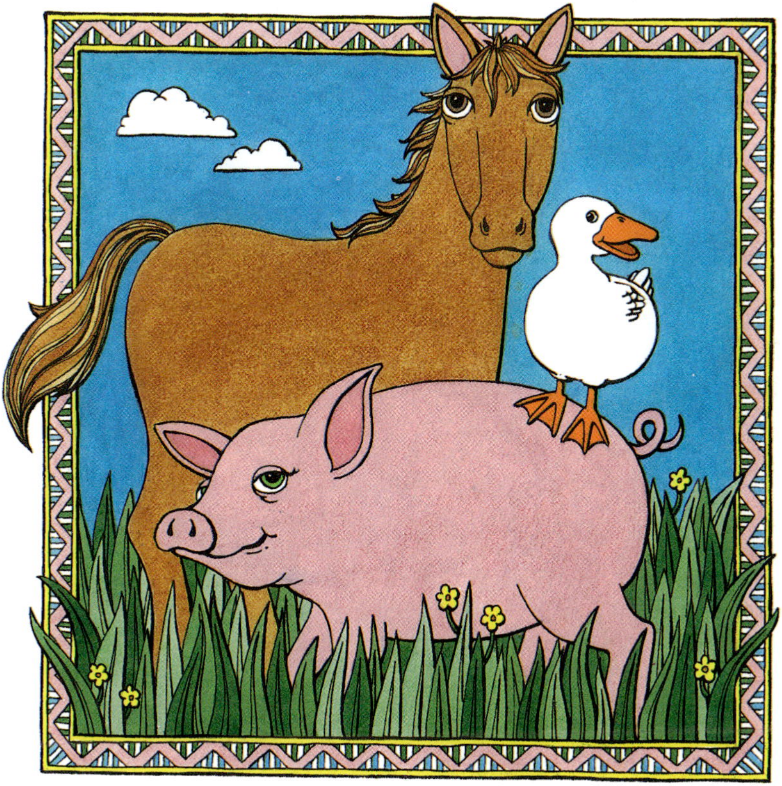

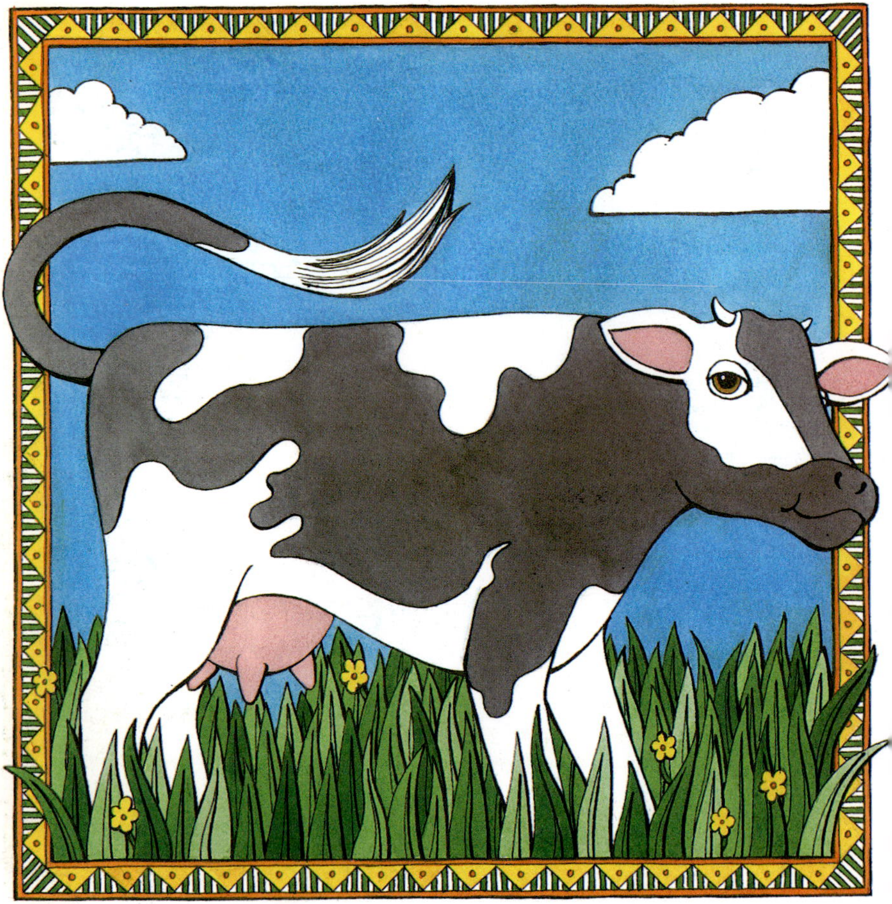

I am a cow.

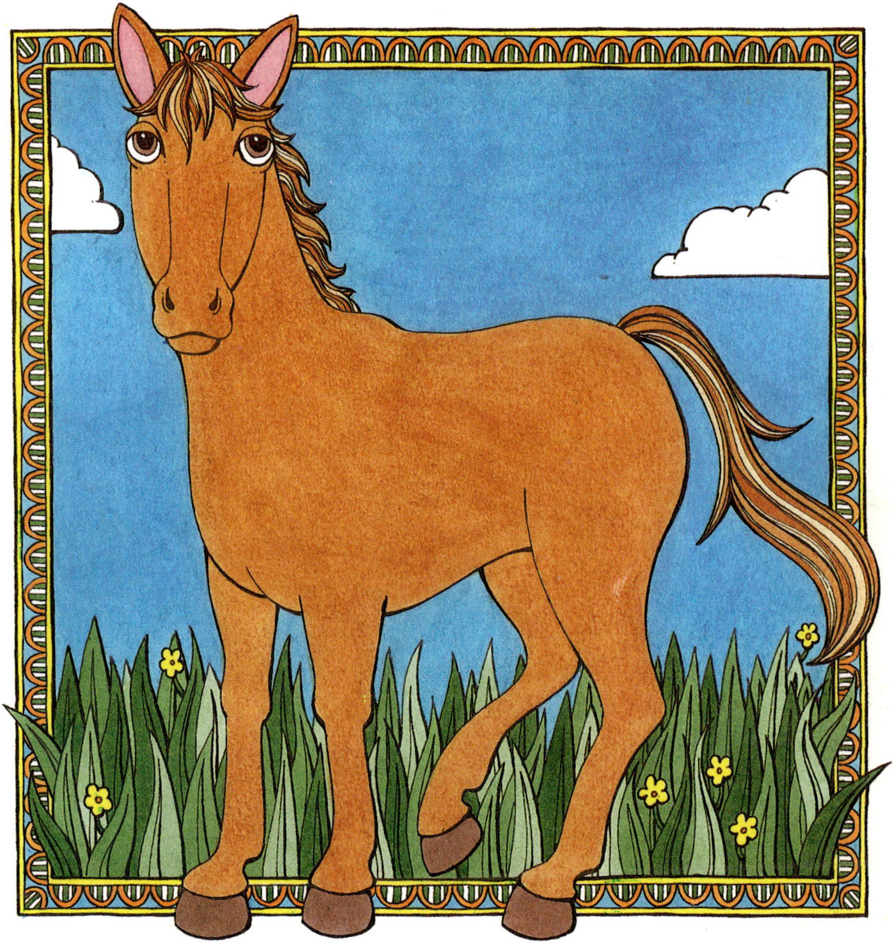

I am a horse.

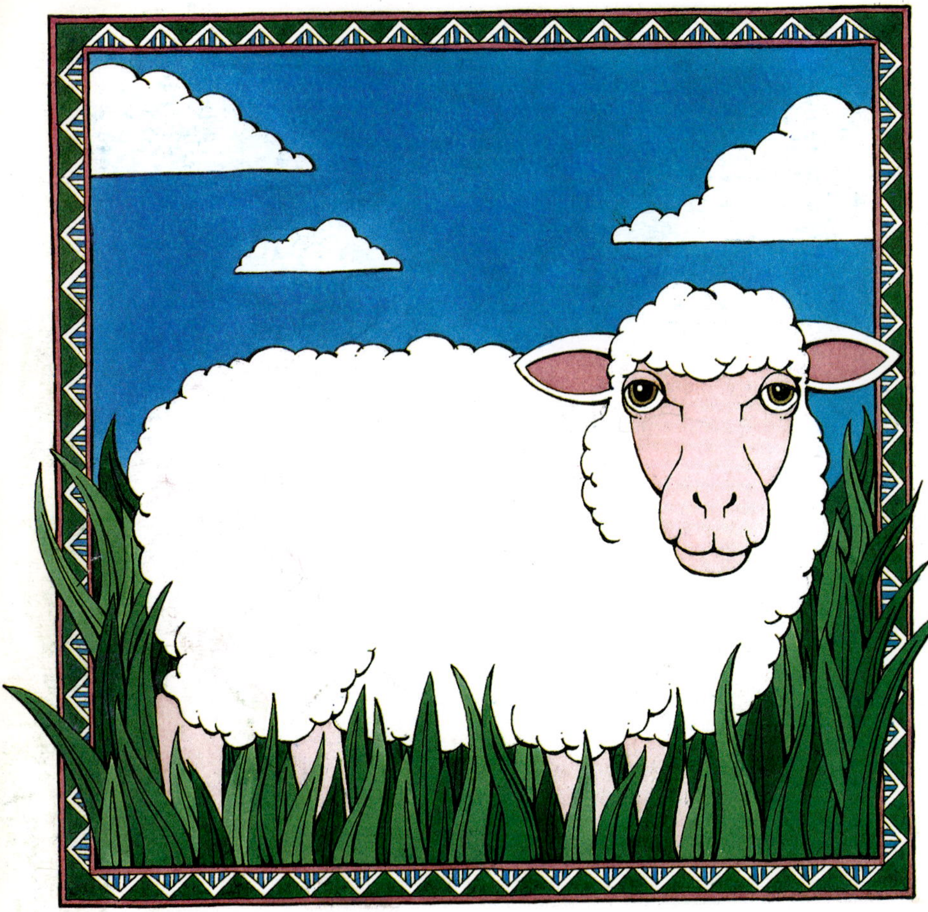

I am a sheep.

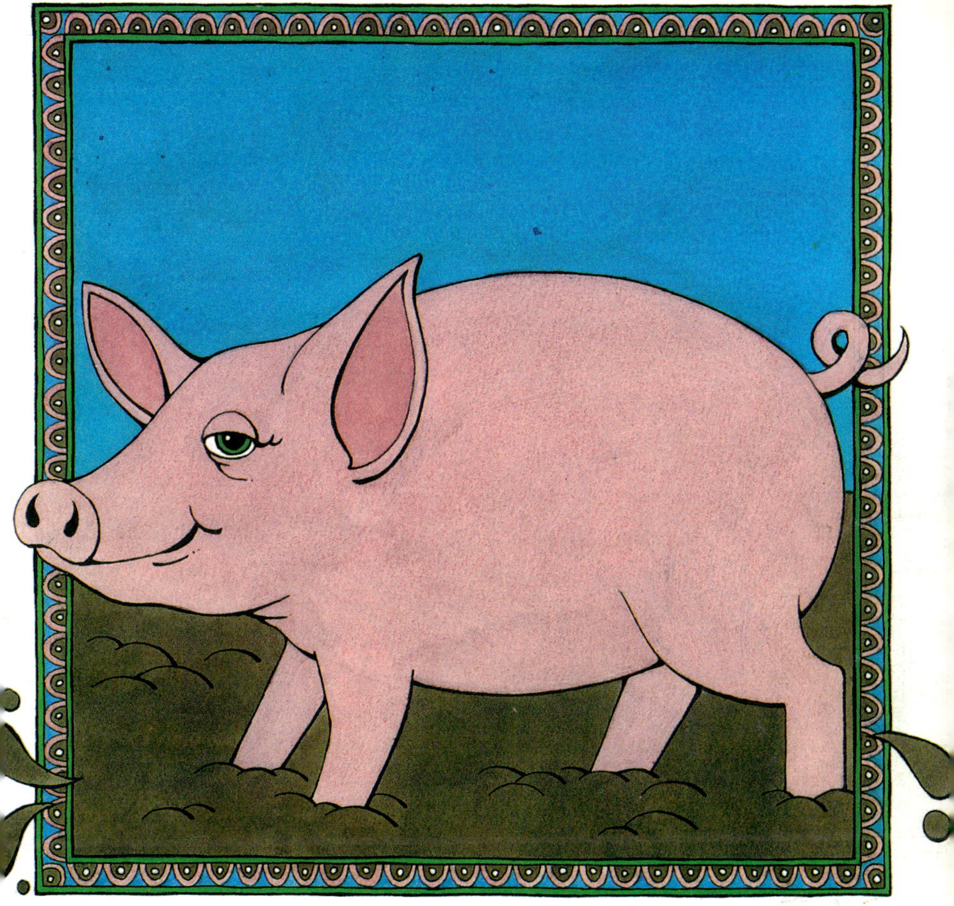

I am a pig.

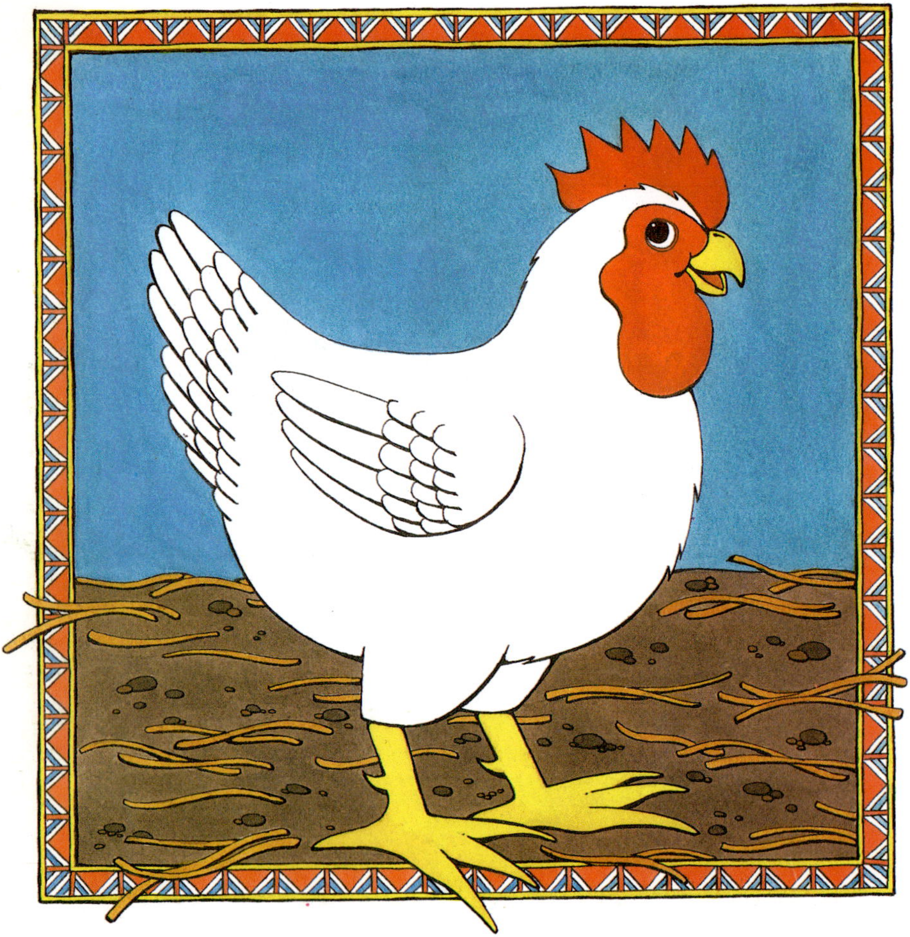

I am a chicken.

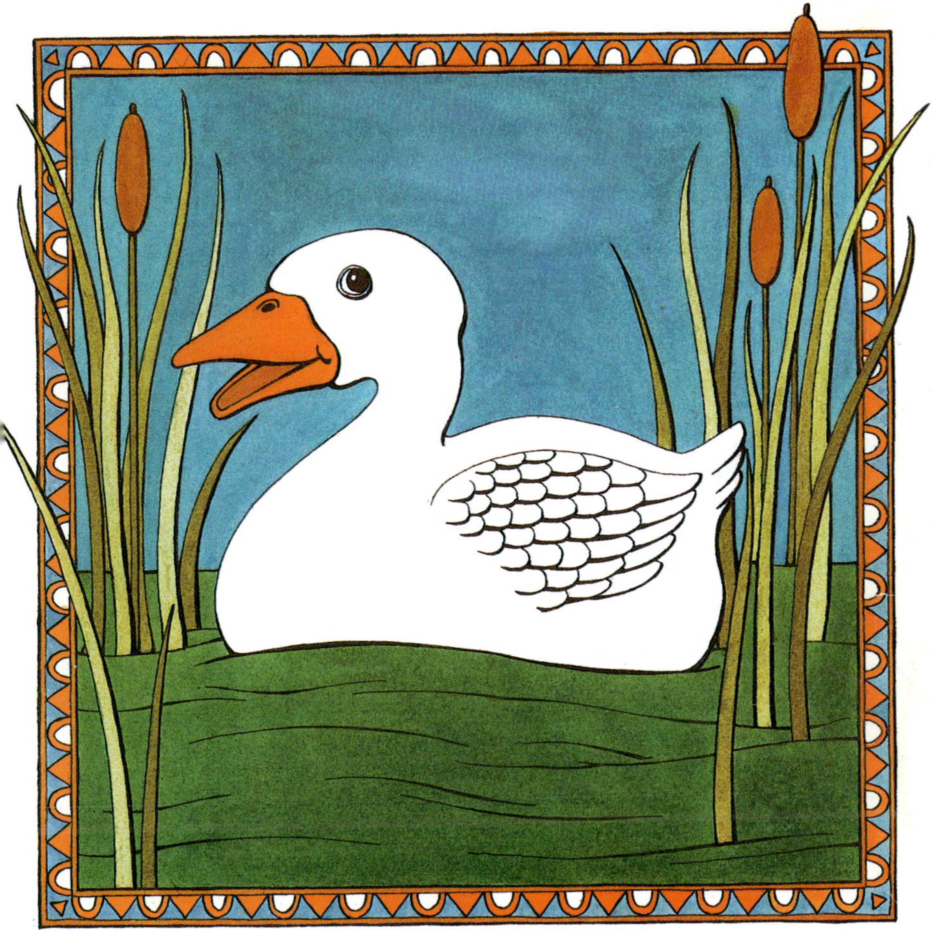

I am a duck.

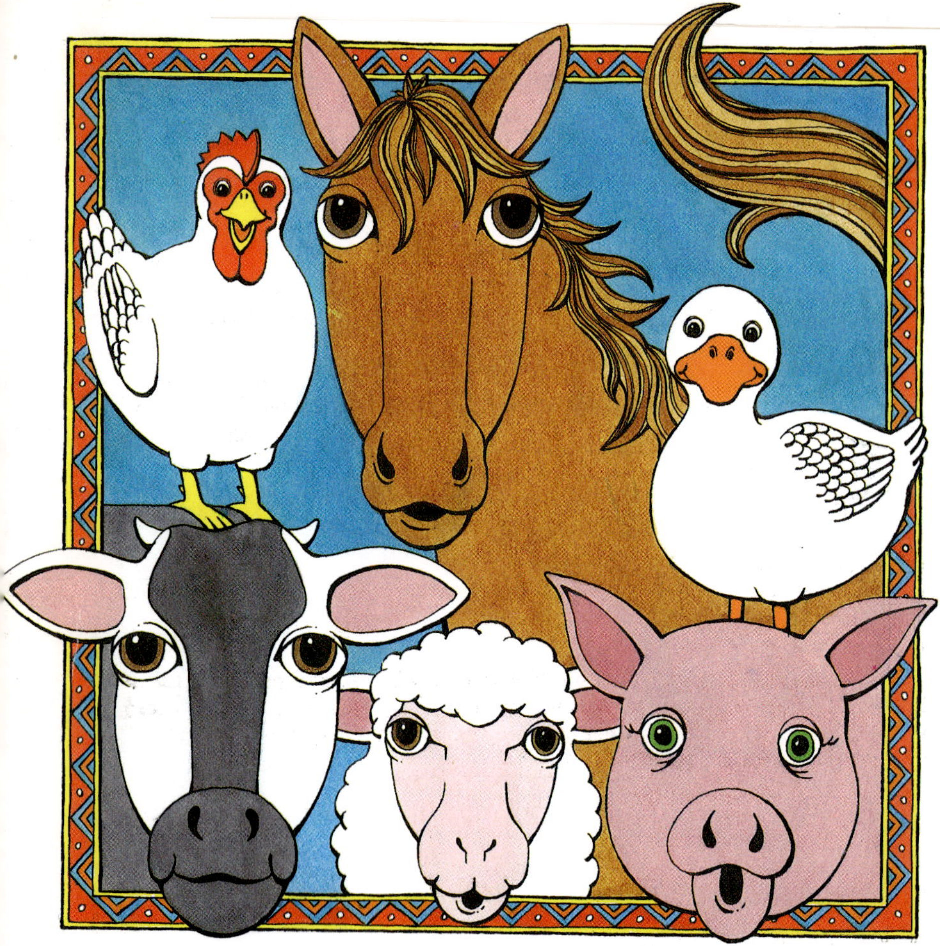

What are you?